STECK-VAUGHN
TOP LINE Math

Decimals

www.HarcourtAchieve.com
1.800.531.5015

Acknowledgments

Editorial Director   Ellen Northcutt
Supervising Editor   Pamela Sears
Senior Editor   Kathy Immel

Associate Design Director Joyce Spicer
Design Team   Jim Cauthron
                               Joan Cunningham

Photo Researcher   Stephanie Arsenault

Cover Art   ©Janet Parke

Photography Credits   p. 6 ©Pitchal Frederic/Sygma/CORBIS;
                               p. 24 Sam Dudgeon.

ISBN 1-4190-0367-4

© 2006 Harcourt Achieve Inc.

All rights reserved. No part of the material protected by this copyright may be reproduced or utilized in any form or by any means, in whole or in part, without permission in writing from the copyright owner. Requests for permission should be mailed to: Copyright Permissions, Harcourt Achieve, P.O. Box 27010, Austin, Texas 78755. Rigby and Steck-Vaughn are trademarks of Harcourt Achieve Inc. registered in the United States of America and/or other jurisdictions.

2 3 4 5 6 7 8 9 10 862 11 10 09 08 07 06 05

Contents

To the Student 2
Setting Goals 3
Pretest 4

UNIT 1
Adding and Subtracting Decimals   6

Overview Lessons 1–4
Understanding Decimals 7
   Lesson 1 Decimal Place Value 8
   Lesson 2 Writing Decimals 10
   Lesson 3 Rounding Decimals 12
   Lesson 4 Comparing and Ordering Decimals . . 14
   Test-Taking Strategy: Use Logical Reasoning . . 16

Overview Lessons 5–6
Adding and Subtracting Decimals 17
   Lesson 5 Adding Decimals 18
   Lesson 6 Subtracting Decimals 20
   Test-Taking Strategy: Make a Table 22

UNIT 1 Review   23

UNIT 2
Multiplying and Dividing Decimals   24

Overview Lessons 7–8
Multiplying Decimals 25
   Lesson 7 Multiplying Decimals by Whole Numbers 26
   Lesson 8 Multiplying Decimals by Decimals . . 28
   Test-Taking Strategy: Use Estimation 30

Overview Lessons 9–10
Dividing Decimals 31
   Lesson 9 Dividing Decimals by Whole Numbers 32
   Lesson 10 Dividing Decimals by Decimals . . . 34
   Test-Taking Strategy: Use Mental Math 36

Overview Lesson 11
Decimals and Fractions 37
   Lesson 11 Changing Fractions to Decimals and Decimals to Fractions 38
   Test-Taking Strategy: Solve a Simpler Problem 40

UNIT 2 Review   41

Post Test 42
Glossary 44
Math Toolkit 46
Review Your Progress . . . . Inside Back Cover

To the Student

Building a solid foundation in math is your key to success in school and in the future. Working with the *Top Line Math* books will help you to develop the basic math skills that you use every day. As you build on math skills that you already know and learn new math skills, you will see how much math connects to real life.

When you read the Overview in this *Top Line Math* book, read the **You Know** and **You Will Learn** sections. As you focus on new math skills, consider how they connect to what you already know.

Pretest and Post Test

Take the Pretest at the beginning of this book. Your results on the Pretest will show you which math skills you already know and which ones you need to develop.

When you have finished working in this book, take the Post Test. Your results on the Post Test will show you how much you have learned.

Practice

Practice pages allow you to practice the skills you have learned in the lesson. You will solve both computation problems and word problems.

Unit Reviews

Unit Reviews let you see how well you have learned the skills and concepts presented in each unit.

Test–Taking Strategy

Every test-taking strategy shows you various tools you can use when taking tests.

Glossary

Each lesson has **key words** that are important to know. Turn to the glossary at the end of the book to learn the meaning of new words. Use the definitions and examples to strengthen your understanding of math terms.

Setting Goals

A goal is something you aim for, something you want to achieve. It is important to set goals throughout your life so you can plan realistic ways to get what you want.

Successful people in all fields set goals. Think about your own goals.

- Where do you see yourself after high school?
- What do you want to be doing 10 years from now?
- What steps do you need to take to get to your goals?

Goal setting is a step-by-step process. To start this process, you need to think about what you want and how you will get it. Setting a long-term goal is a way to plan for the future. A short-term goal is one of the steps you take to achieve your long-term goal.

What is your long-term goal for using this book about decimals? You may want to improve your test scores or you may want to become better at math so you can become a computer programmer.

Write your long-term goal for learning math.

_____

_____

Think about how you already use decimals. Then, set some short-term goals for what you would like to learn in this book. These short-term goals will help you to reach your long-term goal.

I use decimals in my everyday life to
- ☐ compare gas prices.
- ☐ make sure my paycheck is correct.
- ☐ compare times and scores in sports.
- ☐ read digital scales.

My short-term goals for using this book are

_____

_____

Pretest

Take this Pretest before you begin this book. Do not worry if you cannot easily answer all the questions. The Pretest will help you determine which skills you are already strong in and which skills you need to practice.

Write the decimal.

1. 45 and 46 hundredths _____

2. 3 and 71 thousandths _____

3. 16 and 19 thousandths _____

4. 6 hundreds and 5 thousandths _____

What is the value of the underlined digit?

5. 978.2<u>1</u> _____

6. 59.<u>3</u>97 _____

7. 78.7<u>1</u>3 _____

Round each decimal to the nearest tenth.

8. 0.474 _____

9. 17.518 _____

10. 0.995 _____

Compare. Use <, >, or = sign.

11. 0.378 ☐ 0.48

12. 7.379 ☐ 7.37

13. 0.72 ☐ 1.7

Order the decimals from least to greatest.

14. 1.9 0.19 0.109 0.91 _____

15. 47.52 47.500 47.05 47.205 _____

Add or subtract.

16. 6.465 + 143.78 = _____

17. 9.003 + 18.34 = _____

18. 7.45 − 3.76 = _____

19. 32.9 − 6.37 = _____

Multiply or divide.

20. 30.6 × 3 = _____

21. 320 ÷ 0.4 = _____

22. 0.62 × 42 = _____

23. 3864 ÷ 9.2 = _____

Change each decimal to a fraction or fraction to a decimal.

24. 0.75 _____

25. $\frac{7}{10}$ _____

26. 0.9 _____

27. $\frac{3}{100}$ _____

Solve.

28. If 4 yards of fabric cost $10.00, how much does 1 yard of fabric cost?

29. An athlete runs a mile in 8.4 minutes. If he runs at the same speed for 5 miles, how long will it take him?

30. Tonya is filling out a deposit slip at the bank. She records one check in the amount of $217.89 and another for $87.92. What is the total amount of her deposit?

31. If a person has $609.88 in his savings account and withdraws $145.90, how much is left?

UNIT 1
Adding and Subtracting Decimals

Real-Life Matters

You have already been using decimals for years. When you use money, you are actually working with decimals. A decimal point separates dollars from cents. Your car's odometer shows mileage using decimals. Look at the odometer. How many miles has the car been driven?

Real-Life Application

Your friend asks you to buy some gas for her car. You want to get the most gas for her money so you check different gas stations for the lowest price. The first gas station advertises 1.99\frac{9}{10}$ per gallon.

How much will you actually pay for a gallon of gas at this station?

_____

_____

The second gas station has a sign that says 1.98\frac{87}{100}$ per gallon.

How much will you actually pay for a gallon of gas at the second station?

_____

_____

Which gas station has the better price? Why do you think gas stations use decimal numbers instead of whole numbers?

_____

_____

Your friend gave you $15.00 for gas. The amount you paid at the gas station was $12.50. How much change does she get?

_____

Remember, a decimal with the most digits does not necessarily have the greatest value.

Overview • Lessons 1–4

Understanding Decimals

You have learned about whole numbers and place value. You have also learned about fractions. Now you will learn about decimals. A **decimal** is a number with one or more digits to the right of the decimal point. Numbers such as 2.17 and 0.025 are decimals.

Fractions and decimals both name part of a whole.
- A fraction is a whole divided into any number of parts.
- A decimal is a whole divided into 10, 100, or 1000 parts.
- A fraction with the top number smaller than the bottom one is less than 1.

Decimal	Fraction
0.99	$\frac{99}{100}$

Money is a familiar decimal. A bottle of juice may cost $1.20. The decimal point separates the whole number (1) from a number with a value less than 1 (0.20).

$1.00

20 cents

YOU KNOW
- How to read and write whole numbers in standard form
- How to identify the place value of whole numbers

YOU WILL LEARN
- How to identify the place value of decimals
- How to read and write decimals
- How to round and estimate decimals
- How to compare and order decimals

Remember the BASICS

Simplify. If you need to review these skills, go back to the book on fractions.

1. $\frac{10}{100} = \frac{1}{10}$
2. $\frac{20}{100} =$
3. $\frac{4}{10} =$
4. $\frac{500}{1000} =$
5. $\frac{2}{10} =$
6. $\frac{8}{200} =$
7. $\frac{25}{100} =$
8. $\frac{350}{1000} =$
9. $\frac{120}{1000} =$

LESSON 1 Decimal Place Value

Decimal place value is similar to whole number place value. Look at the place value chart. Find the decimal point. Notice that as you move to the left of the decimal point, each place is 10 times *greater* than the place on its right. As you move to the right of the decimal point, each place is $\frac{1}{10}$ times *smaller* than the place on its left.

When reading a decimal, read the decimal point as *and*.

Example

Look at the number 9.756. Identify the value of the underlined digit.

STEP 1 Write the number in the place value chart below.
Write "9" in the ones column, "7" in tenths column, "5" in the hundredths column, and "6" in the thousandths column.

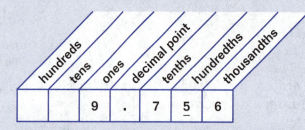

STEP 2 Write the underlined digit and the name of its column.

5   hundredths

In the number 9.756, the value of the underlined digit is 5 hundredths.

ON YOUR OWN

Look at the number 56.142. What is the value of the underlined digit?

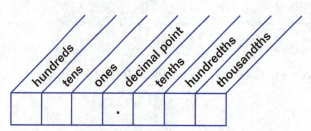

8 LESSON 1

Practice

The zeros to the right of a decimal point have a place value.

Building Skills

Solve each problem by finding the value of the underlined digit.

1. 10.9<u>7</u>8   7 hundredths
2. 67.0<u>0</u>4 _____
3. 0.<u>3</u>1 _____
4. 987.2<u>6</u>5 _____
5. 74.<u>2</u>7 _____
6. 9.85<u>9</u> _____
7. 32.1<u>5</u>3 _____
8. 12.0<u>9</u>8 _____
9. 52.4<u>3</u>5 _____
10. 61.7<u>4</u> _____

Problem Solving

For each problem, circle the correct answer.

11. Max is thinking of a 3-digit decimal. One of the digits is 8 tenths. Circle the number that he is thinking of.

    5.893   5.98   8.67   (6.87)   4.998

12. Julie tried to memorize a secret 5-digit code. She forgot all but one digit, which is 9 thousandths. Circle the number shown below that might be the secret code.

    42.503   9.1805   15.009   13.895   45.958

13. Yana won the 100-meter dash in 10.62 seconds. The second-place runner took 2 tenths of a second longer to finish. Circle the number that shows the second-place time.

    8.62   10.42   10.82   10.24   9.62

14. Read the clues, then decide which 6-digit number is the mystery decimal and circle it.
    - One of the digits is 7 tenths.
    - The digit in the thousandths place is even.
    - The digit in the hundredths place is greater than 3.50.

    234.736   23.783   321.742   783.874   987.367

15. Last season Adrian had a batting average of 0.215. Angel had a higher batting average than Adrian. Circle the number that shows the higher batting average.

    0.213   0.035   0.217   0.025   0.207

LESSON 2 — Writing Decimals

When learning to write decimals, write the numbers in a place value chart. Look at the chart and find the column farthest to the right with a number. The name of the decimal is taken from the name of that column. The name for the number in the chart is 298 thousandths. In standard form it is 0.298. The zero in the ones place tells you that the decimal is less than one.

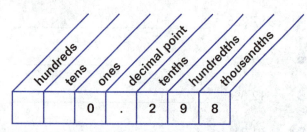

Example

Write 75 thousandths in standard form.

STEP 1 Look at the word after the number. This word tells where to put the last digit in the number.
The word *thousandths* tells you that the 5 will go into the thousandths column.

STEP 2 Write the decimal digits in the place-value chart to the right of the decimal point.
Write 5 in the thousandths column. Write 7 in the hundredths column.

STEP 3 If necessary, add zeros as placeholders to fill space between the decimal point and digits farther to the right.
Write 0 in the tenths place.

STEP 4 Write digits or 0 in the ones, tens, or hundreds place.
This decimal does not have whole numbers. Place "0" in the ones column.

75 thousandths in standard form is 0.075

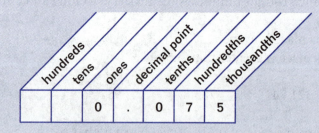

ON YOUR OWN

A bucket holds 12 and 85 hundredths gallons of water. Write the decimal in standard form.

Practice

> When you write a decimal, use a decimal point for *and*.

Building Skills

Write the decimal in standard form.

1. 1 and 465 thousandths   1.465
2. 12 and 79 thousandths   _____
3. 48 hundredths   _____
4. 2 and 7 tenths   _____
5. 9 and 2 hundredths   _____
6. 8 and 14 thousandths   _____
7. 34 and 8 thousandths   _____
8. 698 and 3 hundredths   _____
9. 3 and 5 tenths   _____
10. 325 and 26 hundredths   _____

Problem Solving

For each problem, write the decimal in standard form.

11. Isabel is buying a sack of potatoes that weighs 5 and 2 hundredths of a pound.

    5.02 pounds

12. Ping runs the cross-country trail in her neighborhood every day. The trail is 2 and 4 tenths blocks long.

13. In 1941, Ted Williams of the Boston Red Sox had a batting average of 406 thousandths.

14. A marathon is 26 and 3 tenths miles long.

15. An Internet search engine created the results of a search in 21 hundredths of a seconds.

16. The average rainfall in January for Galveston, Texas is 3 and 26 hundredths inches.

17. A bottle of perfume contains 2 and 6 tenths ounces.

18. A shoelace is about 31 and 3 tenths inches long.

LESSON 3 Rounding Decimals

Rounding decimals is similar to rounding whole numbers. Suppose you want to round 1.13 to the nearest tenth. Look at the number line below. You can see that 1.13 is closer to 1.1 than to 1.2. So, 1.13 rounded to the nearest tenth is 1.1.

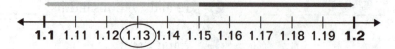

Look at the other numbers on the number line. All of the numbers less than 1.15 round down to 1.1. The number 1.15 and everything greater rounds up to 1.2.

Example

You can also use place value to round decimals.
Round 6.38 to the nearest tenth.

STEP 1 Find the digit in the place value you want to round to and circle it.

STEP 2 Underline the digit to the right of the circled digit.

STEP 3 If the underlined digit is 5 or greater, add 1 to the circled digit. If the underlined digit is less than 5, do not change the circled digit. Finally, drop the remaining digits to the right of the circled digit.

Because 8 is greater than 5, add 1 to the circled digit. Then drop the 8.

When rounded to the nearest tenth. 6.38 is 6.4.

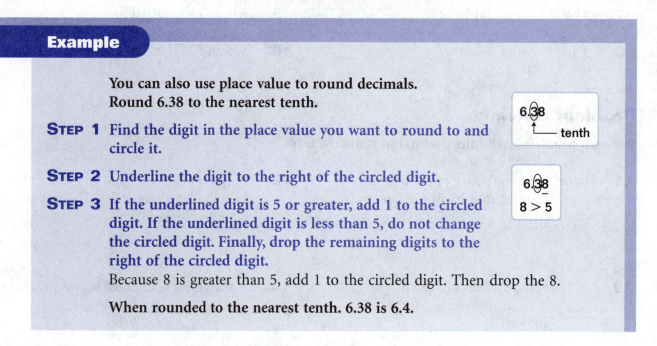

ON YOUR OWN

Round 4.762 to the nearest hundredth.
Use either a number line or place value.

Practice

> If the number to the right is 5 or >5, round up.

Building Skills

Solve each problem by rounding.

1. Round 34.671 to the nearest tenth.

   34.6̂71 → 34.6̂7̱1 → 34.7

2. Round 8.36 to the nearest tenth.

3. Round 143.62 to the nearest tenth.

4. Round 9.256 to the nearest hundredth.

5. Round 6.873 to the nearest hundredth.

6. Round 0.723 to the nearest hundredth.

7. Round 132.4521 to the nearest thousandth.

8. Round 79.9901 to the nearest thousandth.

Problem Solving

Use rounding to solve these problems.

9. Kanya rounds a decimal to the nearest tenth. Her answer is 34.9. Which decimal did she round up? Circle your answer.

   34.09   (34.87)   34.96   34.99   34.00

10. Doli rounds a decimal to the nearest whole number. Her answer is 12. Which decimal could *not* have been the original decimal? Circle your answer.

    12.41   11.987   12.378   11.47   12.9

11. The tadpole you measured in biology class is 3.65 inches long. How long is the tadpole to the nearest tenth of an inch?

12. Tanika's lunch cost $8.53 including the tip. She does not want to wait for change, so she decides to round the amount to the nearest dollar. How much money does Tanika leave?

LESSON 4: Comparing and Ordering Decimals

Look at the place value chart. When comparing decimals with different numbers of digits, you begin by adding zeros to the right of the last digit so that both decimals have the same number of digits.

Start with the whole numbers and then move right to the tenths, hundredths, and thousandths place. Stop when you find two digits in the same column that are different. In the example, there are two different digits in the thousandths place.

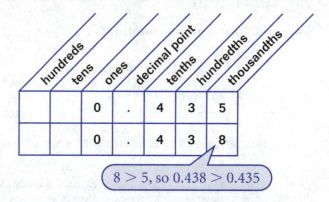

$8 > 5$, so $0.438 > 0.435$

Example

Which decimal is greater, 0.78 or 0.781?

STEP 1 Line up the decimal points. Comparing decimals is easier if both decimals have the same number of places. Add zeros to the end of the decimals if needed.
0.78**0** (Add one zero)
0.781

STEP 2 Compare digits. Start on the left. When you find two different digits, underline them.
0.78<u>0</u>
0.78<u>1</u>

STEP 3 Compare the underlined digits. The decimal with the greater underlined digit is the greater number.
0.78<u>0</u>   0.78<u>1</u>
$1 > 0$, so $0.781 > 0.780$.

$0.781 > 0.78$

ON YOUR OWN

Which decimal is greater, 6.405 or 6.45?

Practice

> < less than
> \> greater than
> = is equal to

Building Skills

Compare. Use <, >, or = sign.

1. 0.50 [=] 0.5
2. 1.4 [ ] 1.45
3. 0.64 [ ] 0.69
4. 7.05 [ ] 7.50
5. 0.4 [ ] 0.400
6. 0.39$\overline{4}$ [ ] 0.394

Order the decimals from least to greatest.

7. 0.7   0.07   0.17   1.7 _____

8. 0.456   0.45   0.5   0.405 _____

Order the decimals from greatest to least.

9. 11.27   1.27   11.2   12.27 _____

10. 0.380   0.387   0.37   0.4 _____

Problem Solving

Use ordering to solve these problems.

11. A red pitcher holds 1.56 quarts of liquid and a green pitcher holds 1.5 quarts. Which pitcher holds the greater amount of liquid?

    > 1.56   1.50   6 > 0, so 1.56 > 1.5

12. In 2002, 4.35 million people visited an amusement park. In 2003, 4.7 million people visited the park. Which year did the park have the greater number of visitors?

13. It costs $13.47 to run an air conditioner for one month. A clothes dryer costs $14.53 for electricity to run for one month and a refrigerator costs $14.65. Which appliance costs the most to use?

14. During June, it rained 0.20 inches in Tucson, Arizona. In San Diego, California it rained 0.07 inches, and Anchorage, Alaska had 1.14 inches of rainfall. Which city had the most rain in June?

TEST-TAKING STRATEGY

Use Logical Reasoning

Sometimes you need to know the order of events to answer test questions. Logical reasoning will help you find the order. Making a chart can help you sort information.

Example

Sylvia, Andy, Ryan, and Beth's times in a swim meet race were 25.6 seconds, 24.6 seconds, 25.1 seconds, and 24.8 seconds. Sylvia finished in less than 25 seconds. Andy finished in less time than Sylvia did. Ryan finished last. What was Beth's time?

	24.6	24.8	25.1	25.6
Sylvia	✘	✓		
Andy	✓			
Ryan				✓
Beth			✓	

STEP 1 Write the names vertically.

STEP 2 Write the times in order from fastest to slowest horizontally.

STEP 3 Read each clue carefully. Use the clues in the problem to find each swimmer's time.
Clue 1: Sylvia's time is less than 25 seconds. Her time could be 24.6 seconds or 24.8 seconds. Put a check mark in the chart next to Sylvia's name under 24.6 and 24.8.
Clue 2: Andy finished in less time than Sylvia. Put a check mark next to Andy's name under the fastest time.
Clue 3: Ryan finished last. Put a check mark next to Ryan's name under the slowest time recorded.

STEP 4 Complete the chart.
You know Ryan swam the fastest (24.6 seconds), Sylvia came in second (24.8 seconds) and Ryan came in last (25.6 seconds). Beth must have come in third. Complete the chart by entering a checkmark for Beth under 25.1 seconds.

TRY IT OUT

Rachel, Tom, Elaine, and Manuel are lined up from shortest to tallest for their class pictures. Their heights are 5.52 feet, 5.82 feet, 5.68 feet, and 5.71 feet. Rachel is the shortest. Tom is over 5.68 feet tall. Elaine is taller than Tom. What is Manuel's height?

Circle the correct answer.

A. 5.52 feet **B.** 5.82 feet **C.** 5.68 feet **D.** 5.71 feet

Option C is correct. Rachel is the shortest, so her height is 5.52 feet. Tom is over 5.68 feet tall, so his height is either 5.71 or 5.82 feet. Elaine is taller than Tom, so Elaine's height is 5.82 feet and Tom's height is 5.71 feet. The only height left is 5.68 feet, so Manuel's height is 5.68 feet.

Overview • Lessons 5–6

Adding and Subtracting Decimals

You know that when you add and subtract whole numbers, you must line up the digits by place value. You use the same rule to add or subtract decimals.

Suppose that the French Club is trying to raise money to take a trip. The club had four events and raised $109.75, $82.10, $111.05, and $97.35. You need to add $109.75, $82.10, $111.05, and $97.35 to find the total amount the club raised.

	hundreds	tens	ones	decimal point	tenths	hundredths
	1	0	9	.	7	5
		8	2	.	1	0
	1	1	1	.	0	5
+		9	7	.	3	5
	4	0	0	.	2	5

When you add or subtract money you add or subtract decimals. In this example, the French Club raised $400.25.

YOU KNOW
- How to add and subtract whole numbers
- How to line up digits with the same place value
- How to read place values in decimals

YOU WILL LEARN
- How to add decimals
- How to subtract decimals

Remember the BASICS

Fill in the empty spaces on the place-value chart. If you need to review these skills, turn to page 6.

NUMBER	HUNDREDS	TENS	ONES	DECIMAL POINT	TENTHS	HUNDREDTHS	THOUSANDTHS	NUMBER WORDS
1.762			1	.	7	6	2	One and seven hundred sixty-two thousandths
		3	2	.	5			
284.73				.				
	3	5	4	.	0	8	1	Three hundred fifty-four and eighty-one thousandths
			0	.	0	7	5	
				.				One hundred twenty-four thousandths

LESSONS 5–6 OVERVIEW

LESSON 5 Adding Decimals

You add decimals in the same way that you add whole numbers.

First, write the numbers so the decimal points line up. If there are empty spaces to the right of the last digit in any number, add zeros as placeholders.

Add 1.539 + 0.53

hundreds	tens	ones	decimal point	tenths	hundredths	thousandths
		¹1	.	5	3	9
+		0	.	5	3	0
		2	.	0	6	9

Add a zero as a placeholder.

Next, put a decimal point in the answer directly below the other decimal points. Then add the same way you add whole numbers.

Example

Add 3.45 + 0.638

STEP 1 Write the numbers so the decimal points line up.

$$\begin{array}{r} 3.45 \\ +0.638 \end{array}$$

STEP 2 Add zeros as placeholders.

$$\begin{array}{r} 3.450 \\ +0.638 \end{array}$$

STEP 3 Put a decimal point in the answer directly under the other decimal points.

STEP 4 Add. Regroup as necessary.

3.45 + 0.638 = 4.088

$$\begin{array}{r} 3.450 \\ +0.638 \\ \hline 4.088 \end{array}$$

ON YOUR OWN

Sam has two wooden boards. One board is 2.5 feet long. The other board is 3.56 feet long. If Sam glues the two boards together to make one long wooden board, how long will it be?

Practice

> Line up the decimal points before you add.

Building Skills

Add. Show your work.

1. 25.43 + 32.7 = **58.13**

    25.43
    + 32.70
    ─────
    58.13

2. 1.598 + 12.4 = _____

3. 7 + 6.89 = _____

4. 3.015 + 7.96 = _____

5. 0.476 + 3.79 = _____

6. 4.109 + 0.47 = _____

7. 8.54 + 2.226 = _____

8. 3.17 + 8.036 = _____

9. 0.211 + 13.5 = _____

10. 56.7 + 12.25 = _____

Problem Solving

Add. Show your work.

11. Hoshi poured 2.7 quarts of water in a bucket. Then, she added 4.09 more quarts. How many quarts of water did Hoshi pour in the bucket?

    2.7 quarts + 4.09 quarts = 2.79 quarts

12. In 2002, 4.5 million tourists visited Alcatraz prison, near San Francisco, CA. The year before, 5.95 million visited. How many people visited Alcatraz in 2001 and 2002?

13. The decorator bought 13.4 yards of fabric to make curtains. He went back to the store and bought 6.98 more yards. How many yards of fabric did he buy in all?

14. The painter bought 15.57 gallons of red paint and 8 gallons of white paint. How many gallons of paint did she buy in all?

LESSON 6 Subtracting Decimals

You subtract decimals in the same way that you subtract whole numbers.

First, write the numbers so the decimal points line up. If there are empty spaces to the right of the last digit in any number, add zeros as placeholders.

Subtract 6.792 − 0.57

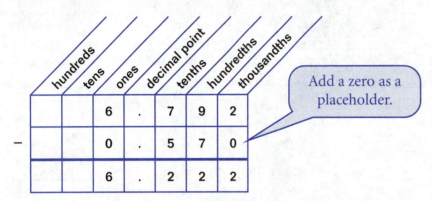

Add a zero as a placeholder.

Next, put a decimal point in the answer directly below the other decimal points. Then, subtract decimals the same way you subtract whole numbers.

Example

Subtract 9.25 − 1.018

STEP 1 Write the numbers so the decimal points line up.

$$\begin{array}{r} 9.25 \\ -1.018 \end{array}$$

STEP 2 Add zeros as placeholders.

$$\begin{array}{r} 9.250 \\ -1.018 \end{array}$$

STEP 3 Place a decimal point in the answer directly under the other decimal points.

STEP 4 Subtract. Regroup as necessary.

9.25 − 1.018 = 8.232

$$\begin{array}{r} 9.2\overset{41}{5}0 \\ -1.018 \\ \hline 8.232 \end{array}$$

ON YOUR OWN

Asha had 29.5 quarts of syrup for ice drinks before the carnival started. She used 18.75 quarts. How many quarts of syrup did she have left?

Practice

> Line up the decimal points before you subtract.

Building Skills

Subtract. Show your work.

1. 14.93 − 2.74 = __12.19__

    14.93
    − 2.74

    12.19

2. 1.874 − 0.91 = _____

3. 7.51 − 6.215 = _____

4. 43.706 − 16.91 = _____

5. 0.879 − 0.68 = _____

6. 4.647 − 2.984 = _____

7. 6.23 − 3.985 = _____

8. 4.42 − 1.28 = _____

9. 0.806 − 0.54 = _____

10. 14.714 − 0.029 = _____

Problem Solving

Subtract. Show your work.

11. Students in the drama department were painting scenery for a play. They had 5.5 gallons of white paint and used 2.6 gallons to paint a winter scene. They need about 2.5 more gallons to finish. Will they have enough paint?

    5.5 gallons − 2.6 gallons = 2.9 gallons

12. Coach Ortiz had 20.75 pints of sports drink for game night. The players drank 14.6 pints. How many pints were left over?

13. As a junior, Kira ran the 200-meter dash in 28.34 seconds. In her senior year, she ran it in 25.22 seconds. How many seconds faster was she in her senior year than in her junior year?

14. One day in August, the Dow Jones Industrial Average, a stock market index, ended the day at 10,179.16 points. On the next day, the index ended at 10,120.24. How many points lower did the index end on the second day?

LESSON 6

TEST-TAKING STRATEGY

Make a Table

Organizing information in a table will help you answer test questions about decimals.

Example

Jamal recorded the highest and lowest temperatures in each month for three months. In which month was the difference in temperature the greatest?

STEP 1 Organize the data in a table.

STEP 2 Find the difference in temperature for each month.

STEP 3 Order the temperature differences from greatest to least.
15.1°F   11.6°F   10.1°F
15.1°F is greater than 11.6°F and 10.1°F.

The temperature difference was greatest in August.

July Low Temp. – 78.1°F
August Low Temp. – 80.8°F
August High Temp. – 95.9°F
June Low Temp. – 64.9°F
June High Temp. – 76.5°F
July High Temp. – 88.2°F

	High Temp. (°F)	Low Temp. (°F)
June	76.5	64.9
July	88.2	78.1
August	95.9	80.8

June: 76.5 − 64.9 = 11.6
July: 88.2 − 78.1 = 10.1
August: 95.9 − 80.8 = 15.1

TRY IT OUT

Gloria deposited her earnings from babysitting, gardening, and tutoring in her bank account. In which job did she earn the greatest amount of money?
Circle the correct answer.

A. gardening

B. babysitting

C. tutoring

DATE	TRANSACTION DESCRIPTION	AMOUNT OF DEPOSIT
7/9	gardening	$10.50
7/12	tutoring	$8.25
7/18	gardening	$9.25
7/24	babysitting	$14.75
7/30	babysitting	$12.25
8/5	tutoring	$15.50
8/11	gardening	$11.75
8/16	tutoring	$13.50
8/20	babysitting	$9.25

Option C is correct. Gloria earned the greatest amount of money tutoring, $37.25.

UNIT 1 Review

Write the decimal in standard form.

1. 45 and 9 tenths _____
2. 12 and 6 thousandths _____

Write the value of each underlined digit.

3. 4.0<u>9</u>8 _____
4. 27.00<u>4</u> _____

Round each decimal.

5. Round 0.15 to the nearest tenth. _____
6. Round 14.32 to the nearest tenth. _____

Compare. Use <, >, or =.

7. 0.89 ☐ 0.9
8. 45.050 ☐ 45.05

Order the decimals from least to greatest.

9. 0.15, 0.105, 0.051, 0.501 _____
10. 0.32, 0.302, 0.032, 3.01 _____

Add.

11. 46.9 + 2.7 = _____
12. 12.405 + 13.282 = _____
13. 21.15 + 196.37 = _____
14. 20.01 + 80.99 = _____

Subtract.

15. 6.56 − 2.793 = _____
16. 82.05 − 25.681 = _____
17. 17.48 − 7.99 = _____
18. 13.78 − 12.7 = _____

19. Anissa has $5.87 and Kate has $9.43. Do they have enough money to buy a CD that is on sale for $14.99?

20. Rafi is a competitive speed skater who can skate 1,500 meters in 193.95 seconds and 1,000 meters in 117.18 seconds. How much more time does it take him to go 1,500 meters?

UNIT 2: Multiplying and Dividing Decimals

Learning to multiply and divide decimals can help you make wise shopping decisions.

Real-Life Matters

A video store has an ad in the window. It reads: *Huge Savings – Buy 3 CDs for only $33.00*. If the regular price of one CD is $11.99, is it a huge savings to buy 3 for $33.00?

You can find the total price of three CDs by multiplying the regular price of a CD by 3. You find that three CDs at the regular price are $35.97. At the sale price three CDs are $33.00. Although you save when you buy three CDs at the sale price, the savings are not that huge because you only save $2.97.

Real-Life Application

What did you do to figure out whether the offer is a good deal?

_____

_____

The same store sells video games. New video games are $29.95 and used ones sell for $14.95. How much would three new games cost?

_____

_____

You have saved $50.00 to buy some used games. How many can you buy?

_____

Would you rather buy four used games or two new games? Explain your choice.

_____

Overview • Lessons 7-8

Multiplying Decimals

Multiplying decimals is almost like multiplying whole numbers. With decimals you have to know where to put the decimal point in your answer.

Look at the box of baseballs. Suppose Coach Griffin wants to buy 12 baseballs. Each one costs $14.49. To find the cost of 12 baseballs, you could add $14.49 twelve times or you could multiply $14.49 by 12.

```
  $14.49  ⟶ factors
×     12
  28 98
 144 9
 $173.88  ⟶ product
```

The cost of 12 baseballs is $173.88.

Baseballs $14.49 each

YOU KNOW
- How to multiply whole numbers
- How to find the place value of a decimal

YOU WILL LEARN
- How to multiply a decimal by a whole number
- How to multiply a decimal by a decimal

Remember the BASICS

Complete the place-value chart. If you need to review these skills, turn to page 8.

NUMBER	TENS	ONES	DECIMAL POINT	TENTHS	HUNDREDTHS	THOUSANDTHS	NUMBER OF DECIMAL PLACES
1.76		1	.	7	6		2
	3	2	.	5	4	7	
84.73			.				
	5	4	.	0	8		
24.963			.				

LESSON 7: Multiplying Decimals by Whole Numbers

Suppose you drive 7.8 miles to and from school every weekday, and you want to find out how many miles you drive in a week. You can add 7.8 five times, but it is easier to multiply 7.8 by 5.

```
 ⁴7.8
+ 7.8
+ 7.8
+ 7.8                ⁴7.8
+ 7.8              ×    5
 39.0      OR      39.0
```

Example

Multiply 28.3 × 6.

STEP 1 Multiply. Ignore the decimal point for now.

```
 ⁴2¹8.3
×    6
 1698
```

STEP 2 Count the number of decimal places in each number.

```
 28.3  ← 1 decimal place
×   6  ← 0 decimal places
 1698  ← 1 decimal place
```

STEP 3 Starting at the right side of the answer, count that number of decimal places to the left, and put the decimal point there.

28.3 × 6 = 169.8

```
 28.3   ← 1 decimal place
×   6   ← 0 decimal places
 169.8  ← 1 decimal place
```

ON YOUR OWN

Lorenzo is making 7 banners for the science fair. He needs 1.4 yards of fabric for each banner. How many yards of fabric does he need in all?

Practice

> Remember to put the decimal point in your answer.

Building Skills

Multiply. Show your work.

1. $9.9 \times 2 = $ __19.8__

   $\begin{array}{r} {}^19.9 \\ \times\ \ 2 \\ \hline 19.8 \end{array}$

2. $7.2 \times 5 = $ _____

3. $4.13 \times 9 = $ _____

4. $61.7 \times 8 = $ _____

5. $0.45 \times 7 = $ _____

6. $27.4 \times 13 = $ _____

7. $1.32 \times 21 = $ _____

8. $12.5 \times 12 = $ _____

9. $60.1 \times 32 = $ _____

Problem Solving

Multiply. Show your work.

10. You are teaching crafts at a summer camp. Nine children want to make yarn dolls. If each doll takes 3.5 yards of yarn, how many yards will you need in all?

    $\begin{array}{r} {}^43.5 \\ \times\ \ 9 \\ \hline 31.5 \end{array}$

11. A popular model of car gets 34.5 miles per gallon. Its gas tank holds 14 gallon. How far could you go on a full tank of gas?

12. Three auto mechanics each work 8.5 hours per day. What is the total number of hours they work per day?

13. Rosario is responsible for ordering supplies for the Chinese restaurant. The 12 soy sauce containers hold 4.5 gallons each and need to be refilled every week. How many gallons of soy sauce should Rosario order?

LESSON 7

LESSON 8 Multiplying Decimals by Decimals

Suppose you want to buy wood to make a frame for a picture. The wood is $2.10 per foot and you need 4.5 feet. To find the total cost of the wood, you could add. However, it is easier and faster to multiply.

$2.10 + $2.10 + $2.10 + $2.10 + $1.05 = $9.45

or

$2.10 × 4.5 = $9.45

Four 1-foot pieces at $2.10 each; 1 half-foot piece at $1.05.

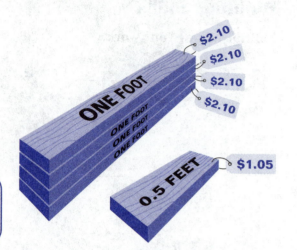

Example

Multiply 5.3 × 2.8

STEP 1 Multiply.
Ignore the decimal point for now.

```
  5.3
×2.8
  424
 106
 1484
```

STEP 2 Count the number of decimal places in each number.

```
  5.3  ← 1 decimal place
×2.8   ← 1 decimal place
  424
 106
 1484  ← 2 decimal places
```

STEP 3 Starting at the right side of the answer, count that number of places to the left and put the decimal point there.

5.3 × 2.8 = 14.84

14.84 ← 2 decimal places

ON YOUR OWN

Rose is making a poster for her science exhibit. It is 2.4 feet long by 1.8 feet wide. What is the area of the poster? *(Area = length × width)*

Practice

> Count the number of decimal places.

Building Skills

Multiply. Show your work.

1. $4.2 \times 1.3 = $ __5.46__

    $$\begin{array}{r} 4.2 \\ \times 1.3 \\ \hline 126 \\ 42 \\ \hline 5.46 \end{array}$$

2. $4.9 \times 0.2 = $ _____

3. $5.03 \times 6.8 = $ _____

4. $8.7 \times 0.13 = $ _____

5. $8.1 \times 0.22 = $ _____

6. $24.1 \times 0.14 = $ _____

7. $1.32 \times 2.4 = $ _____

8. $13.9 \times 2.7 = $ _____

9. $4.8 \times 3.8 = $ _____

Problem Solving

Multiply to solve each problem. Show your work.

10. The weight of a calf increases 4.3 pounds a day. How much weight will a calf gain in 7.5 days?

    $$\begin{array}{r} {}^{2}7.5 \\ \times 4.3 \\ \hline 225 \\ 300 \\ \hline 32.25 \end{array}$$

11. Pistachios cost $4.80 a pound. How much will 3.25 pounds cost?

12. Devon gets paid $9.30 an hour. If he works 25.6 hours, how much will he get paid?

13. Lily is making a travel crate for her dog. The bottom can be no more than 22 square feet. One side is 4.2 feet and the other side is 5.1 feet. To find the area, multiply 4.2 and 5.1. Is the area greater than 22 square feet?

TEST–TAKING STRATEGY

Use Estimation

Estimation can help you decide where to place the decimal point in a product.

Example

Mr. Sanchez bought 22.3 pounds of chicken nuggets for a neighborhood picnic. Chicken nuggets cost $4.79 per pound. How much did Mr. Sanchez spend?

STEP 1 Use compatible numbers to estimate the product.
Compatible numbers are close to the actual numbers but are easier to use.
($\approx$ means *almost equal to*)

$22.3 \approx 20 \quad\quad 4.79 \approx 5$
$22.3 \times 4.79 \approx 20 \times 5$, so $22.3 \times 4.79 \approx 100$.

STEP 2 Multiply.

STEP 3 Use the estimate to place the decimal point in the product.
The estimate is in the hundreds. Put the decimal point to the right of 6, or 106.817.

```
   22.3
  ×4.79
   2007
   1561
    892
 106817
```

STEP 4 Because you are working with money, round your answer to the nearest hundredth.

Mr. Sanchez spent **$106.82**.

TRY IT OUT

Bev's car gets 36.7 miles per gallon in city driving. The fuel tank holds 11.4 gallons. How many miles of city driving can Bev expect if her car has a full tank of gas?
Circle the correct answer.

A. 4.1838 miles   **B.** 41.838 miles   **C.** 418.38 miles   **D.** 4,183.8 miles

Option C is correct. When you use compatible numbers ($36.7 \approx 40$; $11.4 \approx 10$) to estimate the product of 36.7×11.4, the estimate is in the hundreds ($40 \times 10 = 400$).

Overview • Lessons 9–10

Dividing Decimals

Dividing decimals is not much different from dividing whole numbers. It is a matter of learning some simple rules for moving the decimal point.

Look at the box of baseball gloves. Suppose that a full box of gloves costs $96.80. To find the cost of one baseball glove, divide the total cost by the number of gloves in the box.

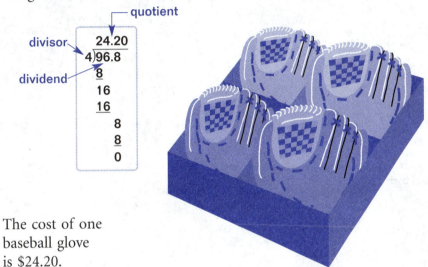

```
          quotient
          ↓
divisor   24.20
      →  4)96.8
dividend  8
          ―
          16
          16
          ―
           8
           8
           ―
           0
```

The cost of one baseball glove is $24.20.

YOU KNOW
- How to divide whole numbers
- How to write decimals

YOU WILL LEARN
- How to divide a decimal by a whole number
- How to divide a decimal by a decimal

Remember the BASICS

Divide.

1. 150 ÷ 6 =

```
     25
   6)150
     12
     ――
      30
      30
      ――
       0
```

2. 204 ÷ 3

3. 1,188 ÷ 9

4. 2,336 ÷ 4

5. 450 ÷ 10

6. 384 ÷ 24

7. 1,170 ÷ 18

8. 1,755 ÷ 65

LESSON 9: Dividing Decimals by Whole Numbers

You use division when you want to separate an amount into equal parts. Suppose you have $13.75 to spend on school lunches for a week. How much can you spend each day?

To find out, divide $13.75 by 5. You have to remember to put the decimal point in the quotient directly above the decimal point in the dividend. You can spend $2.75 a day for lunch.

Example

Divide 25.13 ÷ 7

STEP 1 Divide.
You can ignore the decimal point for now.

```
   3 59
7)25.13
  21
   4 1
   3 5
     63
     63
      0
```

STEP 2 Look at the decimal point in the dividend. Put a decimal point directly above it in the answer.

STEP 3 If the decimal point falls to the left of the first digit in the quotient, place a zero in the ones place. (This step is not needed here.)

25.13 ÷ 7 = 3.59

```
   3.59
7)25.13
  21
   4 1
   3 5
     63
     63
      0
```

ON YOUR OWN

An art teacher has 3.5 yards of fabric. She divides it among seven students for a project. How much fabric does each student get?

Practice

> Remember to put a decimal point in your answer directly above the decimal point in the dividend.

Building Skills

Divide. Show your work.

1. $19.8 \div 2 = $ __9.9__

```
    9.9
2)19.8
   18
   ‾‾
    1 8
    1 8
    ‾‾‾
      0
```

2. $7.2 \div 5 = $ _____

3. $37.17 \div 9 = $ _____

4. $493.6 \div 8 = $ _____

5. $3.15 \div 7 = $ _____

6. $356.2 \div 13 = $ _____

7. $27.72 \div 21 = $ _____

8. $150.6 \div 12 = $ _____

9. $195.2 \div 32 = $ _____

Problem Solving

Divide. Show your work.

10. Kaleesha went on a surfing trip with friends. She had $150.00. If she was gone for 4 days, how much money could she spend each day?

```
      37.50
4)150.00
   12
   ‾‾
    30
    28
    ‾‾
     20
     20
     ‾‾
      0
```

11. Andrew uses 52.5 cups of flour to make oatmeal cookies for a bake sale. If he makes 15 batches of cookies, how many cups of flour does he use for each batch?

12. Natasha earns $163.90 a week working at a health club juice bar. She works 22 hours in a week. How much is she paid per hour?

13. A package of string cheese contains 16.875 ounces of cheese. If there are 15 pieces of cheese in the package, how many ounces does each piece weigh?

LESSON 9

LESSON 10 — Dividing Decimals by Decimals

Dividing a decimal by a decimal is similar to dividing decimals by whole numbers. Now you will have to change the divisor to a whole number before you begin dividing.

Example

Birdseed costs $1.21 for 2.75 pounds. How much does 1 pound cost? Divide $1.21 ÷ 2.75

STEP 1 Set up the problem.

STEP 2 Count the number of decimals places in the divisor. Each decimal has two decimal places to the right of the decimal point.

STEP 3 Move the decimal points as many places as there are decimal places in the divisor. Move the decimal point two places to the right.

STEP 4 Divide. Add zeros as necessary.

STEP 5 Put a decimal point in your answer directly above the decimal point in the dividend. If the decimal point falls to the left of the first digit in the quotient, place a zero to the left of the decimal point.

The birdseed is $0.44 per pound.

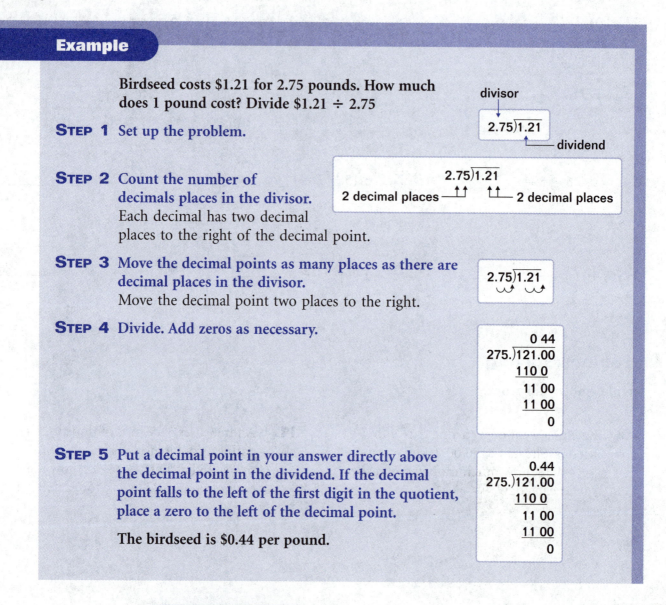

ON YOUR OWN

Manuel bought 4.6 pounds of fresh fish for $14.03. How much did the fish cost per pound?

Practice

> Move the decimal point to the right the same number of places in divisor and dividend.

Building Skills

Divide. Show your work.

1. $367.2 \div 7.2 =$ __51__

   ```
         5 1.
   7.2)367.2
       360
       ─────
        7 2
        7 2
       ─────
          0
   ```
   divisor → 7.2) 367.2 ← dividend

2. $0.48 \div 2.4 =$ _____

3. $9.8 \div 4.9 =$ _____

4. $61.5 \div 12.3 =$ _____

5. $9.72 \div 7.2 =$ _____

6. $356.2 \div 1.3 =$ _____

7. $2.100 \div 0.56 =$ _____

8. $8.4 \div 0.42 =$ _____

9. $5.856 \div 0.32 =$ _____

Problem Solving

Divide. Show your work.

10. A sandwich shop buys smoked cheese for $3.25 per pound. The shop spent $48.75 for cheese. How many pounds of cheese did the shop buy?

    ```
            15
    3.25)48.75
         32 5
         ─────
         16 25
         16 25
         ─────
             0
    ```

11. Josh wants to make new covers for several chairs. He has 34.5 yards of fabric and needs to use 5.75 yards for each chair. How many chairs can he cover?

LESSON 10 35

TEST-TAKING STRATEGY

Use Mental Math

You can use mental math to answer test questions about dividing with decimals.

Example

A dollar bill is about 0.004 inches thick. How many dollar bills are in a stack of bills 36 inches high?

STEP 1 Start with a fact you know.
Using whole numbers, you know that 36 ÷ 4 = 9.

STEP 2 Count the number of decimal places in the divisor (the second number in the equation) by moving the decimal point until you reach 0.004.
There are three decimal places in the divisor, so you move the decimal point three places.

STEP 3 Put the same number of zeros to the right of your answer.

There are 9,000 dollar bills in a stack of bills 36 inches high.

TRY IT OUT

Paper for a printer is stored in a basket 27 centimeters high. Each sheet of paper is 0.009 centimeters thick. How many sheets of paper fill the basket?

Circle the correct answer.

A. 30　　　　　　　　B. 300　　　　　　　　C. 3,000　　　　　　　　D. 30,000

Option C is correct. It takes 3,000 sheets of paper to fill the basket because 27 ÷ 9 = 3, so 27 ÷ 0.009 = 3,000.

Overview • Lesson 11

Decimals and Fractions

Decimals and fractions both show part of a whole. Look at the row of seats in this movie theater. Five out of 10 seats are filled. We can use the fraction $\frac{5}{10}$ or the decimal 0.5 to show how many seats are filled. Sometimes it is easier to use decimals to solve problems. Other times fractions are easier. Knowing how to change fractions to decimals or decimals to fractions will help you solve problems.

YOU KNOW
- How to read and write decimals
- How to read and write fractions
- How to write equivalent fractions with denominators of 10 or 100

YOU WILL LEARN
- How to change fractions to decimals
- How to change decimals to fractions

Five Tenths $\left(\frac{5}{10}\right)$, or 0.5, of these seats are filled.

Remember the BASICS

Write the word name for each fraction or decimal.

1. $\frac{4}{10}$ _four-tenths_
2. 0.3 _____
3. $\frac{8}{10}$ _____
4. 0.9 _____
5. $\frac{9}{100}$ _____
6. 0.02 _____
7. $\frac{43}{100}$ _____
8. 0.62 _____
9. 0.75 _____

Write each fraction as an equivalent fraction with a denominator of 10 or 100.

10. $\frac{4}{5} = \frac{8}{10}$
11. $\frac{1}{2} =$
12. $\frac{6}{50} =$
13. $\frac{9}{25} =$

LESSON 11 Changing Fractions to Decimals and Decimals to Fractions

In 2001, 7 out of 10 high school students were able to graduate. You can write this relationship as $\frac{7}{10}$. You can also express $\frac{7}{10}$ as a decimal, 0.7. Changing decimals to fractions and fractions to decimals is easy, once you learn the simple rules.

Example

Change $\frac{4}{5}$ to a decimal.

STEP 1 Find an equivalent fraction with a denominator of 10 or 100. To find an equivalent fraction, you must multiply the numerator and denominator by the same number.

$$\frac{4}{5} \times \frac{2}{2} = \frac{8}{10}$$

STEP 2 Write the name of the equivalent fraction. Then write the decimal.

The fraction $\frac{4}{5}$ can be written as the decimal 0.8.

$\frac{8}{10}$ ⟶ eight-tenths ⟶ 0.8

Example

Change 0.52 to a fraction.

STEP 1 Write the word name for the decimal. The word name for 0.52 is fifty-two hundredths.

STEP 2 Write the word name as a fraction.

STEP 3 Simplify if possible.

0.52 can be written as the fraction $\frac{13}{25}$.

fifty-two hundredths ⟶ $\frac{52}{100}$

$\frac{52}{100} = \frac{13}{25}$

ON YOUR OWN

Six out of 50 people are left-handed. Write the fraction $\frac{6}{50}$ as a decimal.

The world's smallest fish, the stout infantfish, is 0.28 inches long. Write the decimal 0.28 as a fraction.

Practice

Reduce all fractions to lowest terms.

Building Skills

Write each fraction as a decimal. Show your work.

1. $\frac{1}{5}$ 0.2

2. $\frac{3}{4}$ _____

3. $\frac{31}{50}$ _____

$$\frac{1}{5} \xrightarrow{\times 2} \frac{2}{10} = 0.2$$

4. $\frac{7}{25}$ _____

5. $\frac{9}{10}$ _____

6. $\frac{7}{8}$ _____

Write each decimal as a fraction.

7. 0.08

8. 0.23

9. 0.03

$$0.08 \to \text{eight hundredths} \to \frac{8}{100} \div \frac{4}{4} = \frac{2}{25}$$

10. 0.6

11. 0.4

12. 0.75

Problem Solving

Change between fractions and decimals. Show your work.

13. Ken Marimoto got $\frac{6}{25}$ of the votes in the election for mayor. Write this fraction as a decimal.

$$\frac{6}{25} \times \frac{4}{4} = \frac{24}{100} = 0.24$$

14. A survey showed that $\frac{7}{20}$ of adults never heard a hip-hop performance. Write this fraction as a decimal.

15. A report stated that 0.55 of the people in the U.S. have used the Internet. Write the decimal as a fraction.

16. One serving of chicken noodle soup gives you 0.04 of the vitamin A you need every day. Write the decimal as a fraction.

LESSON 11

TEST–TAKING STRATEGY

Solve a Simpler Problem

When you solve problems involving fractions, it's easier to change fractions to decimals before you begin to solve the problem. You can use mental math to quickly change a fraction to a decimal.

Example

Batting average is the average number of hits a baseball player would get if the player were at bat 1,000 times. The chart shows the number of hits 5 players got when they were at bat 40 times. What is Leo's batting average?

Player	Number of Hits in 40 At Bats
Pam	9
Leo	11
Jake	7
Vera	5
Chen	7

STEP 1 Use the chart to find the number of hits Leo got. The chart shows that Leo got 11 hits.

STEP 2 Write 11 hits out of 40 times at bat as a fraction.

$$\frac{\text{number of hits}}{\text{times at bat}} \rightarrow \frac{11}{40}$$

STEP 3 Write a fraction equal to $\frac{11}{40}$ with a denominator of 1,000.

$$\frac{11}{40} \times \frac{25}{25} = \frac{275}{1,000}$$

STEP 4 Count the number of zeros in the denominator. There are 3 zeros in 1,000.

STEP 5 Move the decimal point in the numerator the same number of places to the left as there are zeros in the numerator.

$$275 \rightarrow 0.275$$
$$\frac{275}{1,000} \rightarrow 0.275$$

Leo's batting average is 0.275.

TRY IT OUT

The chart above shows that two players have 7 hits out of 40 times at bat. What is their batting average?

Choose the correct answer.

A. 0.125   B. 0.140   C. 0.175   D. 0.225

Option C is correct. $\frac{7}{40} = \frac{175}{1,000} = 0.175$.

UNIT 2 Review

Multiply.

1. 7.4 × 3 = _____
2. 37.8 × 21 = _____
3. 2.07 × 14 = _____
4. 4.3 × 2.1 = _____
5. 4.06 × 3.9 = _____
6. 3.4 × 0.52 = _____

Divide.

7. 6.24 ÷ 4 = _____
8. 86.8 ÷ 7 = _____
9. 427.7 ÷ 14 = _____
10. 0.864 ÷ 2.7 = _____
11. 1.596 ÷ 0.21 = _____
12. 64.48 ÷ 5.2 = _____

Change fractions to decimals or decimals to fractions.

13. $\frac{2}{5}$ _____
14. $\frac{1}{4}$ _____
15. $\frac{1}{2}$ _____
16. $\frac{9}{25}$ _____
17. 0.12 _____
18. 0.3 _____
19. 0.7 _____
20. 0.8 _____

Solve each problem.

21. Amy makes $9.90 per hour as a trainee for a trucking company. How much does she earn working 35 hours per week?

22. Butternut squash was selling for $1.90 per pound. Decarlo chose one that weighed 3.2 pounds. How much did the squash cost?

23. Three park rangers had 103.2 pounds of gear to transport on foot. They divided the gear up equally. How many pounds did each ranger carry?

24. The Winan family collected 50.75 gallons of sap from their maple tree to make maple syrup. The buckets for collecting the sap hold 2.5 gallons. How many full buckets of sap did they collect?

Post Test

Take this Post Test after you have completed this book. The Post Test will help you determine how far you have progressed in building your math skills.

Write the decimal.

1. 49 and 31 hundredths _____

2. 4 and 7 thousandths _____

3. 22 and 3 hundredths _____

4. 7 hundreds and 75 thousandths _____

What is the value of the underlined digit?

5. 145.2̱1 _____

6. 23.4̱09 _____

7. 0.03̱3 _____

Round each decimal.

8. Round 0.681 to the nearest tenth _____

9. Round 3.115 to the nearest hundredth _____

10. Round 28. 872 to the nearest tenth _____

Compare. Use <, >, or = sign.

11. 0.49 ☐ 0.491

12. 7.043 ☐ 7.04

13. 0.22 ☐ 2.2

Order the decimals from least to greatest.

14. 4.4; 0.44; 0.404; 0.41 _____

15. 33.57; 33.50; 33.07; 33.207 _____

Add or subtract.

16. 8.235 + 121.11 = _____

17. 13.167 + 28.94 = _____

18. 7.05 − 3.89 = _____

19. 67.9 − 6.092 = _____

Multiply or divide.

20. 21.9 × 5 = _____

21. 19.95 ÷ 7 = _____

22. 0.34 × 27 = _____

23. 4.50 ÷ 0.5 = _____

Change each decimal to a fraction or fraction to a decimal.

24. 0.25 _____

25. $\frac{8}{10}$ _____

26. 0.3 _____

27. $\frac{12}{100}$ _____

Solve each problem.

28. Chen spent $135.17 at the grocery and $25.87 at the gas station. Round both numbers to the nearest dollar and show about how much money Chen spent.

29. If a person takes $150 to the grocery store and spends $136.12, how much money is left?

30. Amir has four pieces of fabric of different lengths. They are 1.9 yards, 1.09 yards, 2.89 yards, and 1.85 yards. Order the yardage from shortest to longest.

31. An athlete runs a mile in 9.2 minutes. If he runs at the same speed for 5 miles, how long will it take him?

32. Chantal bought two items at the sporting goods store. He bought a fishing pole for $65.25, and a tackle box for $23.67. How much did he spend for both items?

33. If you eat 1 cup of spicy tomato soup, you will get $\frac{1}{10}$ of your daily requirement of sodium. Write the fraction as a decimal.

Glossary

column (page 8)
a vertical line of numbers

compatible numbers (page 30)
numbers that are close to the original number, but rounded so as to make it easier to use in problem solving

decimal point (page 7)
separates a whole number from a decimal

decimal (page 7)
a number or part of a number that is less than 1

denominator (page 38)
the bottom number in a fraction

digit (page 6)
one of the ten symbols used to write numbers
0 1 2 3 4 5 6 7 8 9

dividend (page 32)
the amount being divided

$$\begin{array}{r} 24.20 \\ 4\overline{)96.80} \end{array} \leftarrow \text{dividend}$$

division (page 32)
an operation that separates an amount into parts. The symbols ÷ and $\overline{)}$ show division.

divisor (page 32)
the number you divide by

divisor
$$\downarrow \begin{array}{r} 24.20 \\ 4\overline{)96.80} \end{array}$$

equivalent (page 38)
the same in value

estimation (page 30)
to arrive a reasonably close answer to an exact number

factors (page 25)
the numbers you multiply

$$\begin{array}{r} 28.3 \\ \times\ 6 \\ \hline 169.8 \end{array} \leftarrow \text{factors}$$

fraction (page 37)
a part of a whole or a group

hundredth (page 8)
a decimal with two places to the right of the decimal point

multiplication (page 24)
repeated addition. The symbol × shows multiplication.

numerator
the top number in a fraction

place value (page 8)
the value of an individual digit depending upon its location within a greater number

place value chart (page 8)
shows the value of each digit in a whole or decimal number, by displaying each digit's location (tenths, hundredths, etc.)

place value system
number system in which the place, or position, of a digit in a number tells you the value of the digit in that number

product (page 25)
the answer to a multiplication problem

$$\begin{array}{r}28.3\\ \times\ 6\\ \hline 169.8\end{array}\leftarrow \text{product}$$

quotient (page 32)
the answer to a division problem

$$\begin{array}{r}24.20\leftarrow \text{quotient}\\ 4\overline{)96.80}\end{array}$$

remainder
the amount left over in a division problem

rounding decimals (page 12)
approximating the value of a decimal number to make it easier to work with

ten thousandth (page 8)
a decimal with four places to the right of the decimal point

tenth (page 8)
a decimal with one place to the right of the decimal point

thousandth (page 8)
decimal with three places to the right of the decimal point

Math Toolkit

Place Value Chart

You can use this chart to help you read and write decimals.

thousands	hundreds	tens	ones	decimal point	tenths	hundredths	thousandths
				.			

You can use this place value chart when adding or subtracting decimals.

thousands	hundreds	tens	ones	decimal point	tenths	hundredths	thousandths
				.			
				.			
				.			